A So Sophisticated Publication

MOMENTS IN LOVE

Reflections through Poetic Expressions

K. LOWERY MOORE

So Sophisticated Publications
Adult Literature with a K*I*S
(Keepin' It Sophisticated)

Also by K. Lowery Moore

When I'm Loving You, a Novel

So Sophisticated Publications
P.O. Box 23002
Washington, DC 20026-3002

ISBN -13: 978-0-9795333-2-7
ISBN -10: 0-9795333-2-5

Cover and Interior Designed by
The Writer's Assistant
www.thewritersassisant.com

Dedication

*This collection of poetry is dedicated to women
of all ethnic backgrounds and the men who
love us unconditionally.*

$\mathcal{C}$ONTENTS

$\mathscr{C}$ONTENTS
(Continued)

$\mathcal{C}$ONTENTS
(Continued)

FOREWORD

As I prepare this collection of poetry, I smile! I smile because I am finally doing something that I absolutely love. I also smile because I have met some really amazing poets and spoken-word artists along my journey, who continue to inspire me; I am forever grateful.

I've been writing poetry since the mid-eighties, when I was about twelve years old. However, my spoken-word journey started in April of 2006, when I decided to share a poem entitled, "For My Mother," that I wrote in honor of what would have been my mother's sixty-fifth birthday. I was at the Phish Tea Café, which was located on H Street in the Northeast quadrant of Washington, DC. Since then, I've enjoyed sharing my poetry with others around the Washington, DC Metropolitan Area. Especially at the H Street Martini Lounge with my Chocolate City Soul Family. Oh how I miss those Monday nights!

This collection of poetry that I've entitled, *Moments in Love: Reflections through Poetic Expressions,* will take you through my personal journal of what I believe it means to love and be loved. You will also witness my love for family and my love for life in general. I simply love life and I love being me!

Enjoy,

K.

"Some see crying as a sign of weakness, but I see it as an act of strength. I am strong because I cry."
— K. Lowery Moore

"Crying is like taking your soul to the laundromat."
—Lyfe Jennings

MOMENTS IN LOVE

Reflections through Poetic Expressions

Untitled

Speak your poetry
Softly into my ear
Saturate my mind
With the intimate thoughts
I love to hear

How can I be your muse?

SELF-LOVE

THE STRENGTH OF A BLACK WOMAN

A lot of strong, black women are single
because there has been an assumption
that since we are independent,
we don't need a man for nothing
Now we all know that is not necessarily true,
so let's clear up this misconception
if that's what being a strong, black woman means to you

Being a strong, black woman doesn't mean
you no longer have to open my door,
or make sure I'm inside the house before driving off,
even if it's not dark outside
It also doesn't mean we can't be submissive
if we find someone we want to submit to
We don't all suffer from angry woman syndrome
that's why I'm admitting this to you

However, being a strong, black woman does mean
one who realizes she is already complete
You can't complete what's already whole
Now what you can do, with the proper compatibility,
is nourish her soul
You'll notice a strong, black woman because she walks
with confidence and has a style and flair of her own
She has a mature attitude and a silent way of saying,
"Damn it, I'm grown."

She's sassy, seductive and you can't touch her self-esteem
She can raise her sons, work fulltime, finish her degree
and still pursue her dream

A strong, black woman gave birth, not once but twice,
with no epidural or any other anesthesia
So now giving birth to each and every one of her dreams
will be a simple procedure
And being a single mother,
she understands what it means to sacrifice
There is no doubt she will go without
to give her children a good life

A strong, black woman knows a few failed relationships
shouldn't make her bitter
And she doesn't have to convince any man
why he should be with her
He'll just know off the break that she is a Godsend
'Cause he'll be constantly thinking, damn where has she been?
In DC, baby, but now I reside in Maryland, PG County
So stop asking where I've been and just be glad you found me

A strong, black woman can compliment another woman
on her hair, shoes, or purse
'Cause although that woman may look good,
she knows it doesn't affect her self-worth
And any woman that's intimidated
because you think there is a shortage of good black men
Need to change her contact lenses or wipe off her glasses
and look again; they are all around us
Now you may need to overlook your height requirement
or your questions on investing

I'm not saying I'm not guilty myself
because I too am learning my lesson

A strong, black woman realizes homeownership
can be achieved without being someone's wife
I'm not saying that wouldn't be nice,
it's just not a must for some of us
Even when she's struggling,
she will still manage to hold it down
Because she knows with God in her life,
that situation will soon be turned around
She doesn't look to her family or friends for validation
And she will extract anyone from her life
that causes too much complication

Most importantly, a strong, black woman had to realize,
a stray bullet that could have killed her or left her paralyzed
didn't have to paralyze her life
And, yes, the fact that bullet hit less than an inch from her spine,
nearly destroyed her mind, because she couldn't help but to think,
"Why did this happen to me, what did I do?"
You know what you see on the news
but never think it would be you

Well, that strong, black woman stands before you today
when today I could have just been a memory
But I stand before you today,
professing that every challenge is some kind of lesson
So take every test and use it to grow
You're not always supposed to know
the "how comes" and the "what fors"
Who knows what prize lies behind those closed doors?

You know the saying, when one door closes, another will open
And to all my sistas, I am just hoping
You realize all that you are, all that you can be
Continue to be strong through any adversity
Discover your purpose, the reason God put you on this Earth
Always remember, only you determine your self-worth

Embrace the amazing strength that has been given,
from our foremothers before us
Because simply put, we are **Black Women**

WORDS OF ENCOURAGEMENT:

I chose to start with this particular poem, "The Strength of a Black Woman," because I have realized that in order to love someone else, you have to first love yourself. As a strong, black woman, I've had to embrace my strengths and accept my flaws. Ladies, we have to have a strong sense of ourselves and realize that having a man doesn't make us complete. If you are suffering from low self-esteem, then you need to get to the root of that issue and deal with it accordingly. We have to love ourselves and be comfortable with ourselves, before we can pursue a healthy, loving relationship.

Family Love

MEMORIES

pitter-patter of small feet
innocent eyes
joyful laughter
chubby thighs
i love you mommy
before a kiss goodnight
love your children
hold them tight

before long
they will be grown
with a family
all their own
pleasant memories
make them last
our precious babies
grow up so fast

A Mother to Her Sons

(Inspired by the poem, "Mother to Son"
by Langston Hughes)

Look, y'all, we don't have it like that
I work hard to feed the both of you
And put clothes on your back
To keep a clean, comfortable roof over your heads
All I'm asking is for you to clean up your rooms
And make your own beds

Sometimes y'all make me want to pull my hair out by the root
I don't want to step on another toy
Or tell you to tighten your belt loop
I know it doesn't make any sense right now to you
But there is an advantage of going to a private school

Plus, I'm sacrificing to pay your tuition
If I get another call from the teacher or principal,
You might come up missing
I have already told them if they have to call me again
They better call for police back up before they let me in

I know y'all think I yell and fuss all the time
But this world is not friendly
So you better get something positive on your mind
I want you to realize all of your potential
Without going through some of the things I've been through
You can draw, so expand on that ability
And you can be an actor, with all that drama
You've been giving me

Trust that there is not much I wouldn't do
I want nothing but the best for the two of you
I'll be right there if ever either one of you fall
And one day you will acknowledge,
"My mother wasn't crazy after all."

ℱOR MY MOTHER
Ernestine Lowery Moore (1941-1983)

Today, and every day, I know you are smiling down on me
And I hope you are proud of the woman I've turned out to be
All that I've done and all that I do
Mama, is in the honor of you

You are the source of my strength to keep me striving for the best
I admired you so, you made motherhood seem effortless
Never complaining, putting your children's needs
In front of your own
I just wish you were here to see how we've grown

All these years have been so hard without you here
Especially on Mother's Day, I wish you could be near
Your picture hangs on my wall to soothe me when I'm sad
Plus your grandsons can see what a beautiful mother I had

But again, I know you're in Heaven smiling down
I would just prefer to have you around
Mama, sometimes I need you,
Especially when the world is not so friendly
But I always live by the values you've instilled in me

To always be strong and walk with my head held high
Carry myself like a lady and never be afraid to cry
To always have dignity and a sense of self respect
Because when all else fails, that's all you have left

So, Mama, as you can see, your baby girl is okay
And in my heart you will always stay

I STILL STRUGGLE

As a little girl, I suffered a tremendous tragedy
I was ten years old when my mother was taken away from me
Who would have known she would leave so soon—a heart attack
And no amount of tears could ever bring her back
So to cover my pain, I put pen to paper
Constantly asking God, why did He have to take her?
With every accomplishment, over and over, I cried
Nothing could seem to ease my pain inside
I want her to see the phenomenal woman I've become
I wanted her to be here for all the things I have done
I need her to tell me how proud she is of me
But I stop pleading because I know that will never be
So, again, I'm angry and I still struggle

Judging from the outside, you may think I've got it going on
Not realizing there are times I wish I was never born
I'm still torn, struggling with the feelings of abandonment
It's not that my mother died, it's just the way she went
Then one day something amazing happened, God sent me a sign
I heard a voice saying, "My child why are you crying?"
A feeling of inner peace would soon appear
My God told me, your mother is always near
Although she is not physically here, she has never left you
She has been there for everything you have been through
The birth of your children, she was right there
So you have to stop thinking that life isn't fair
I made you strong, so I had to test your belief
And it pains me to see I've caused you so much grief
But I had to prepare you for your calling
You are still standing when you could have easily fallen
I have chosen you for a special purpose

Nothing you have done in your life is worthless
You may not see it now, but it is all for reason
I encourage you to always keep on believing
I need you to motivate and uplift
Have faith in Me because I gave you that gift
Just know your mother looks down on you with a smile
And she whispers, *my Lord I am so proud that is my child*

PASSIONATE LOVE

YOU

Up until now, all of your advances I tried to resist
I would walk by you like you did not exist
Knowing damn well you were the man I wanted to be with
Considering our situation, I didn't want to put too much
In jeopardy
But now here you are, under the covers with me

When you leave, your cologne lingers and I question,
How could a woman ever reject you?
'Cause all day long I couldn't wait to get next to you

The way you kiss and caress me, it drives me crazy
It's ironic because before you even spoke to me,
I pictured myself being your lady
That's why I would walk by you several times a day
I sensed you were checking for me the same way

Remember the first night you just held me in your arms
I would look into your eyes
You said you didn't mind just chillin'
However your erection suggested otherwise
But yet and still we just chilled
With you, I manage to smile
When tears have been the norm for a while
Unfortunately, that's what a lonely heart will do
But I can put that all behind me because now I have YOU!

ALL I NEED

All I need is to be held
And gently caressed
Kissed all over
And slowly undressed
Handled with care
By my Nubian brotha
Soulfully unite
As we embrace one another

The feel of your flesh
Against my naked skin
The warmth of my body
Wants to welcome you in
But right now all I need
Is for you to hold me
Tightly in your arms
Because I've been so lonely

Just Hold Me

just hold me
one more time
to help ease my mind
so much heartache and pain
i can't see the rain
through my tears
i'm having my own storm
so all i'm asking
is for you to
just
hold
me
once more

EMOTIONS IN ANTICIPATION

Our interactions are so far and few
But I do look forward to every time I see you
We're just like those two ships that pass each other in the night
Because most of the time it just seem like
Whenever you're coming, I'm leaving
And when I see you unexpectedly, it feels like I'm not breathing
Because you take my breath away
And that's hard for a woman like me to say

I normally don't express my feelings
Because most men don't read the warnings
Fragile, breakable, handle with care
'Cause see that's my heart and it's very costly to repair
So, to avoid all that, I just keep it out of harms way
With a note attached, emotionally unavailable
Come back some other day

But somehow, with you, I feel a little more at ease
I always enjoy the text messages that are sent as a tease
When we do speak, it's always nice to just hear you
Although I would rather be near you,
And no, sweetheart, I don't fear you
I fear love and I swear I don't want to fall
But if you could see the smile on my face whenever you do call

Thoughts of you leave me fantasizing
And sometimes those thoughts become more erotic
Than you can imagine
When that happens, I get up,
Write those thoughts down and I get such a rush

Reading it over later, I make myself blush
I can't believe the feeling I get from a simple hug
As I anticipate the first time we make love

IMAGINE

Imagine being stranded on a deserted island
And all we have is each other
We would need to come up with interesting ways
To entertain one another

I would dance for you
And maybe sing you a song
Provide you with adult entertainment
In nothing but my thong

I would recite you poetry
Straight from my heart
Write you a story about my hero
And you would play that part

I would perform a skit
We all need drama, from time to time
I would give you a full body massage
When you want to just rest your mind

I would provide you comfort
When you start to miss your friends and family
I would be your sex slave
And let you have me any way you wanted me

I would be there to listen
When you needed to talk
I would be your quiet companion
When you wanted to hold hands and take a walk

I would tell you a few jokes
When you needed a good laugh
I would wash you up
If we found a stream to take a bath

I would be your nourishment
When you needed to feed your soul
I would be yours forever
To have and to hold

LUSTFUL LOVE

CHOCOLATE DREAM

Summer of 1995

I've known you for such a short time
Although longer it seems
My thoughts of ecstasy involves you
Because you are **my chocolate dream**

There's nothing like a piece of chocolate
Between my *lips*
Enjoying every bit
Do you get my drift?

If not, take a few moments to think
But here's a hint just in case
I like the taste of sweet chocolate
Down below my waste

Hmmm, how I love chocolate
Whether it's candy, cake, or even ice cream
But in all honestly, I'd rather have you
My chocolate dream

The color of your skin
Dark brown and smooth
For you I'd give up my favorite chocolate bar
If I had to choose

It's hard for me to believe I'm willing
To give up my favorite, a Twix
But I'll come running to you
When I need a chocolate fix

Some women say chocolate is a substitute for sex
And whether or not it's true
For all the chocolate in the world
I would not give up having sex with you

But I've only known you for such a short time
Although longer it seems
And I don't think you really understand
What it means to be **my chocolate dream**

ℱREAKY STATE OF MIND
Summer of 1995

A freaky state of mind
That's what you put me in
My lust for you
Comes from deep within

But my attraction to you
Is more than sexual
I'm mentally captivated
So I'm sure our friendship can grow

As we get to know one another
I'm willing to bet
You will never regret
The day the two of us met

When I first saw you
I instantly knew
I wanted to get to know you
Intimately…

If I want to experiment
And try something new
You said not to hold back
Just call on you

You've shown me so much
Now I want to see more
Don't be surprised
When I'm knocking on your door

Because one thing is true
I can be spontaneous too
When I'm in a freaky state of mind
There's no telling what I will do

LOST LOVE

$\mathcal{I}$N CASE YOU'RE WONDERING

Alone with my thoughts and plenty time to spare
I often wonder why you can't be there
Instead of asking you, I draw my own conclusions
How foolish?
I often wonder how you feel about me
I don't know if I will like your answer, so I just let it be
Again, how foolish of me?

Well in case you are wondering
My idle moments are filled with thoughts of you
The way we make each other laugh and the freaky things we do
How you make up what I call my four C's of good lovin'
Chemistry, communication, and constant cummin'

There's no one I'd rather be with than you
And when you aren't physically there, oh you're still there, boo
But in my mind, and it's amazing
How the mind and body works together
If you relax and allow yourself to be free,
You feel me?

Okay, let's take a brief moment to reminisce;
Do you remember our first kiss?
The way you were pulling me close and I would playfully resist

Remember how you said getting to know me
Brought back that high school feeling?
And how you find those white pants I wear so appealing

Our conversations then grew into a serious stimulation of the mind
Sweetheart, what you and I have is rare and very hard to find
An intellectual connection where two souls intertwine

Now you haven't actually said how you feel about me
But that's okay, you'll get your turn, today's my day
To tell you all the things that's been going on in my head
Things that a long time ago should have been said
How I'd go to bed wishing you were there
Wake up wishing you were there
And when we make love—hmmmm, I won't go there

Because I know how you like your privacy
But see this is what you bring out of me
Just wanting to tell everybody

Well I've said all of this to say
You are the one I call when I'm having a good day
The one I turn to for comfort when a bad day never seem to end
My best friend and I love you!
In Case You're Wondering

PERSONAL NOTE:

When I wrote this poem, "In Case You're Wondering," I was struggling with telling someone very special how I felt about him. I think he was also struggling with sharing his feeling with me. I thought by putting my feelings on paper, it would help me let him know that I loved him. Unfortunately, he has never heard or read this poem. Distance separated us and not only did I not gain the man I love, I lost one of my best friends in the process.

I encourage everyone to tell people how you feel about them. I know it's hard to do that because they might not feel the same way. However you will never know if you don't have the courage to express your feelings.

Thoughts in My Head

As I think back, you were probably one of the best things
That ever happened to me
While some women dismissed your confidence as arrogance
I stepped to you anyway even when I thought
I didn't have a chance
I was so drawn to how your suits hung
And curious as to how you were hung underneath
From the first moment I laid my eyes on you,
I knew you were someone I had to meet

A man that has himself together, I was further impressed
You had me cleaning up my credit and trying to figure out
How I could invest
Believe it or not, I feel as though I'm a better woman
Because of you
Although at times I didn't think I was even good enough for you
I felt so insecure and unsure if you were going to appreciate
My inner qualities
Then I thought to myself one day, I'm just going to be me

There was so much going on, confusing thoughts clouded my head
I couldn't think clearly, trying to understand something you said
But all you said was, "Do you love me?"
I wasn't sure so I decided to ignore you
Walking away was probably the hardest thing I ever had to do
I don't know if I made the right decision
But it was necessary to sort out my feelings

LESSON LEARNED:

What I've learned from the situation represented in "Thoughts in My Head" is there will be some people who may look good to you, but may not be the one for you. Therefore, it may be necessary to step back from the situation and analyze exactly what you are feeling to make sure it's love instead of infatuation or admiration.

WHAT HAPPENED TO OUR LOVE?

Once upon a time I had you in my life
Plans to have your child and to be your wife
We even had plans as to where we would live
Back then we had so much love to give
All of a sudden, things started going wrong
It just seems like we couldn't get along
It got to the point where every day we'd fuss
I guess a future together was never promised to us
But in the beginning it seemed so right
We'd be together all day and on the phone all night
Exchanging the words, I love you
In a year or two ready to say I do
I just don't understand why it all had to end
And the saddest part is we're not even friends
I really can't figure what the problem was
So tell me, what happened to our love?

Well, as time goes on, all wounds heal
I'm still in pain after our ordeal
I have a permanent reminder and what's done is done
But as a single mother, I'm raising our son
Now don't get me wrong, I don't regret he's here
It might be better though if you were near
All I ever wanted was to have a family
It seems that dream has been ruined for me
Everyday I still wonder what is was
That divided two people so much in love

In Memoriam:

The poem, "What Happened to Our Love," was written in 1995 to my son's father, Anthony "Tony" White. Our son, Antonio Jamal, was born in 1993. I just knew Tony and I would be married after Antonio was born, but that never happened. We were so young though. Unfortunately Tony passed away in 1997. I'm glad that before he died, I made peace with our situation by writing this poem and letting him know that no matter what, I didn't have any hard feelings against him. What pains me the most is, my son never got to know his father. So please everyone, love like today is your last day!

MOMENTS IN LOVE:
NOT....

VICIOUS CYCLE OF LOVE

Can somebody tell me why love is necessary?
I don't know either because I am so very
Tired of "I like you" and "you like me" but "you live with her"
So I leave you alone only to have you blowing up my phone
Talking 'bout we can make it work
How you figure that, Cletus?
Life is stressful enough so I swear I don't need this
So then I meet him and he's fed up with love too
Can't shake his *"crazy"* so he don't know what to do
So I go back to him and nothing has changed
After all this time, it's the same ole same
Get up and get high and it's not even noon yet
But damn he's fine so somehow I have no regrets
So I ride that situation out until I feel it needs to end again
Then I decide to kick it with him, but
He has tendencies to also like men…
Now I'm trying to figure out where the hell I'm going wrong
And like Ne-Yo, I don't want to hear another stupid love song
It's a vicious cycle and I don't know how much longer I can take it
I don't know if I can be patient enough to break it

GROW UP

There used to be a time
When a booty call was just fine
If my sons were not home
Oh, it was on
I was even alright
If you didn't spend the night
As a matter of fact I preferred you didn't stay until morning
That way I didn't have to listen to your ass snoring
These days I need more than a little maintenance
This here is not just for when you need to bust, oh trust
I'm still feeling you but you need to step up your game
I've grown up and matured, it's time for you to do the same!

𝒱ENTING

Brotha, you were honking at my ass
From halfway down the street
So that let's me know right there
It's not me you want to meet
You hadn't even seen
What my face looks like
Seems to me you're only concerned
That my jeans fit right
You say I look like the wifey type
But you don't even know me
And that shit you talking
Is really starting to blow me
You want to know why
I got this frown on my face
'Cause I'm wishing you ain't say shit
To me in the first place
So now you're cursing me out
Calling me bitter and such
Well tell that to a bitch

Who gives a fuck!!

SIDE NOTE:

Sorry, I just needed to get that one off my chest!

LOVE THAT MAY NEVER BE...

Am I Alone?

As I write these words
I'm struggling with the fact
I'm in love with someone
Who doesn't love me back
Many nights spent crying,
Trying to understand this situation
That I'm facing

Am I alone?

WORDS OF COMFORT:

Many times when we are going through a heart break, we feel that we are alone. Believe me, you're not. I'm learning to be honest about my feelings no matter how crazy it sounds to other people. Honesty can be the best therapy. Now the healing process can begin.

DECISIONS

The way you make me feel is wrong, my brotha
Because the reality is, you still belong to another
I understand you say your divorce is almost final
But how do I know she won't be back
Because if I realize you are a good man,
She may actually begin to realize the same thing
And want you to once again wear that wedding ring
Then what would I do, I'm in love with you?

Being the family man that you are
I know you would want to do what's right
But look at all the drama that it brings to your life
Is it worth the fussing and fighting
that end with you sleeping in another room?
I want to say something
But I don't know if it's safe to assume
Given the opportunity, I think you would stay for your kids
But ask yourself is a loveless marriage
What a happy home is?
I'm sorry, but I can't continue to fill that void
And I'm getting annoyed with this situation I put myself in
I can't even fault you
Whenever I saw the sadness in your eyes
I took it upon myself to come to your rescue
I wanted to help you through your pain
And help you regain your confidence as a black man, my hero
Always know that I am here for you
It bothers me to see all you allow yourself to go through
You shared with me the message she left calling you
All kinds of worthless bastards and no good nigga

So the way I figure, it's time for you to move on
Even if it's not with me,
Don't you see, the way you live is not healthy
Now I don't know all that you've done
Because it's always three sides
However, to me nothing will ever justify
Badmouthing a father to his child
That's where I draw the line

But see sometimes as women,
We don't appreciate the good qualities that a man posses
Nevertheless, we are quick to stress
When we think he's less than his best
Instead of putting him down we need to uplift him
It disturbs me to see what happens
To most of our good black men
I've seen women put men through some unnecessary hell
You're one of those men, baby I can tell

I see the good man that you are
However, as women, we all have a different definition
Trust me, deep down inside
I want to give you whatever you've been missing
Right now time is not on our side
Yes, I do love you; that is something I could never hide
Understand this is hurting me
Probably more than it's hurting you
But please, you have to let me go,
For now it's the best thing to do

Why Couldn't He?

He felt good to my body
But he wasn't good for my soul
I never understood
The kind of hold
He had over me

For so many years
I've cried so many tears
Wondering what is wrong with me
Why couldn't he love me,
The way I deserved to be?

LOVE FOR ZION

LET'S TALK POETRY

Let's talk poetry
Your place or mine
Burn incense, candles
Pour a couple of glasses of wine
Take our shoes off and relax
Massage each other's mind
I say one line
And you say the first thing that comes to your mind

Let's talk poetry
But first, let me straddle you
We're gonna still talk poetry
Because I am feeling you
A man that's not afraid to express
What he's feeling, I'm impressed
I wanna talk poetry
After I undress

I just wanna give you a little inspiration
From the moment I first saw you,
I already had my motivation
I think this could be a serious work of art
The poetry we'd make together
But before we start

Let's get you comfortable
Now isn't that better
You all relaxed
And me I'm getting wetter

We can take a break
If that's what you want to do
And I'll finish this poem
When I'm through sexing you

$\mathcal{S}$HOW AND TELL

I've been wondering what it would be like to be close to you
Just the two of us, face-to-face, alone at my place
I've been fantasizing about what it would be like to straddle you
Look into your eyes, kiss you softly
First on your lips, then on your neck, then on your chest
And don't worry, for you, I won't neglect the rest
I also want you to explore my body
Every inch of me, slowly, show me how you do
Because I am so into you
So, I've been wondering what it would be like for you to be in me
Stroking deeply, damn, freak me baby, on these silk sheets
Tasting me will be a treat
Don't you know how well chocolate goes with caramel?
So, I was wondering, are you up for a game of show and tell?
But I can show you better than I can tell you
What I've been wanting to do to you!

YOUR WORDS

Your words move me, soothe me…massage my mind
Kiss the back of my neck and then slowly kiss down my spine
Caress my hips, thighs and I don't want it to stop
So I turn myself over to let your words start again from the top
Your words kiss my lips, my breast and on down to my navel
I don't think you understand how your words got me
Ready, willing, and able
Your words have been like some kind of massage therapy
If your words got me like this,
I can't imagine what you would do to me

Your words move me, soothe me… Is this really poetry?
In and out my ear again, again and again
Naw, your words are making love to me
I know words are powerful but damn this is new to me
How is this happening?
Your words have satisfied me and provided pleasure
This moment I will always treasure because never
Has anyone's words given me this sensational feeling
I wish could last forever

CAN I HAVE YOU TONIGHT?

Can I have you tonight?
I know you can feel this chemistry between us
But neither one of us wants to make the first move
But one of us is going to have to
Because you've teased me enough with your words
And I'm ready for you to please me in ways unheard
Let's not talk about who we have or our pasts
Let's just make love and enjoy each other tonight

I need you to satisfy this yearning, I can't take it anymore
And I'm learning to go after what I'm longing for….You
This attraction is strong so what's wrong with sexing me tonight
Well, I'm assuming that's a yes and I'll be willing to bet
Why? Because you haven't left yet
Look at you trying to act all hard, I mean you're hard I see
So quit playing with me

Well, I'm going to make a move so you just relax
While I take off your shoes and those slacks
I can't even believe you're trying to fight this affection
With that kind of erection, and don't worry I have protection
All sizes, colors, flavors
That reminds me; let's see what's up with the strawberry one later
Look at me because I'm serious
And I know you are curious
So let's just make love tonight
Alright?

$\mathcal{S}$OUL MATE

We communicate to each other without saying a word
Your thoughts speak to me although words are not heard
Though this may sound absurd to some,
Others know exactly what I mean
Whenever I'm near you, it's like I'm living in a dream
And I don't want to wake up

From the moment you sat down next to me,
I knew there was something between us
I've learned to trust my instincts
Because they are more than just…gut feelings
Even if we don't act on our feelings
It's no question the chemistry is there
But not acting on our feelings,
The question is, would that be fair?

I've tried to play it off but I really can't hide it
Not to think about you, baby, I've tried it
But every time you walk by me or come near me
I swear my heart skips a few beats

And believe me, it's not easy dealing with this situation
Neither one of us needs this complication
Because you want to be faithful to her
While I want to be faithful to him
If we aren't faithful to ourselves first, does anyone really win?

At night, whether or not I'm alone, I would rather you be there
I don't care *how* she is there for you

I don't care about *what* he does for me
Can't you see, your soul speaks to my soul
And you can't get a deeper connection
This is more than simple affection

And before you say it, it's not even about sex
You know that's not the mission, that's not what this is
It's much deeper than that and, as a matter of fact,
My feelings for you have reached a depth, until now, unknown
And although I'm grown,
I'm standing here with a schoolgirl crush

So I must tell you, it's not okay that you have her
And I am with him
Understand I'm not pressuring you but we also cannot pretend
It's very real, how we both feel
So let's just enjoy this like our favorite dance
But think about it, nothing we do is simply by chance
We are where we are for a reason

And in each season of our lives, God knows what He is doing
Most of the time, we fail to listen
So ask yourself, your relationship, what are you missing?
The answer may very well be…your soul mate

YOUNG LOVE

A Love Like Mine

Sitting in my room, all by myself
Thoughts of you and no one else
I tell you boy, I love you so
And I promise to never, ever let you go
If we ever fell apart I don't know what I'd do
I never loved any boy like I love you
The time we spend, I wish we'd spend together
And when we kiss, I wish it last forever
If all goes well, we will never part
I love you because you're such a sweetheart
Every time I think of you
All the things that we've gone through
I'm glad to say, we survived it all
Now the love that we have stands out proud and tall
And I don't think no one will ever find
A love like mine

A love like mine is very special indeed
He is there when it's love I need
I miss him a lot when he's not with me
I feel real special whenever he kisses me
It's something about the way he holds me tight
That makes me wish he'd hold me all night
I just can't wait to be with him
All alone when the lights are dim
Holding hands, kissing and hugging
And he's giving me all his tender loving
When the time comes everything will be right
Making love by candlelight

I'm all his and he's all mine
I can't wait 'til our souls combine

Everybody needs someone special, you see
And he's that special someone for me
We both know our love is so strong
No one on this Earth can prove us wrong
Nobody can deny the feelings that we share
He cares about me and he knows that I care
I just can't help it, I love him so much
Only he can provide that special touch
I will never listen to what friends and family may say
The bond that combines us won't fade away
Forever and ever 'til the end of time
I will always have this love of mine

TRUE STORY:

I had to put this poem, "A Love Like Mine," in my book. I wrote this for a high school sweetheart. You couldn't tell me anything about our relationship. I swore up and down that he was going to be my husband. I know my sisters both remember. They tried to tell me that was just the beginning of me falling in love. But no, I didn't want to hear it. However, he was truly a sweetheart. Although it was a teenage love, I will never forget him. You see it's been almost twenty years and he's still on my mind. I'm not sure where he is these days, but I really hope life has treated him well.

TEENAGE LOVE

This poem deals with a girl and a boy
Who brought each other happiness and so much joy
The love that was shared was thought to be strong
As it turned out, it was not real all along
I loved this boy with all my heart
That he loved me just as much is what I thought
It seems he had other things on his mind
Tears fell from my eyes as I wrote these lines
Y'all just don't know, it's tearing me up inside
These feelings I have for him are so hard to hide
Too young for a commitment and no love was made
I just didn't expect for our love to fade
This relationship just crumbled apart
As if it was over at the very start
Now I sit here in so much confusion,
Wondering if our love was just an illusion
However, over time I realized what is was
A Teenage Love

POSSIBLE LOVE

COULD THESE BE?

Look into my eyes
tell me
you want me
Intimate thoughts
taunt me
tease me
Vivid visions
please me
Could these be
more than fantasies?

Admiration to Conversation

When I first saw you,
I remember saying to myself,
Now that is a good-looking man
At that moment I did not realize
An innocent compliment would
Turn into secret admiration

Honestly, it is true,
If you are involved with some else
I will sincerely understand
Although it would be a pleasant surprise
If a young lady like me could
Accompany you in conversation

INTERESTING STORY:

There is an interesting story behind this poem, "Admiration to Conversation." In 1995, there was a guy who I wanted to meet, so I wrote him this poem. I didn't know this guy at all, but I felt confident enough to take it to his office and give it to him. I actually stood there while he read it. We ended up having a romance that lasted for several years and a friendship that still exists today.

*C*HECKING FOR YOU

I tried to focus so you wouldn't notice
I was checking for you, hoping you were checking for me too
When you would move your lips to speak,
Your words appeared to be on mute
As I thought to myself, *he is so cute*
I was also visualizing other ways those lips
Could be put to good use
I should not have let my thoughts wander so far
But by the end of this day, I must know who you are

REKINDLE

Some say we should leave the past in the past
There's a reason why back then the relationship didn't last
I believe in what I call, the boomerang concept
If you let someone go and it was meant to be,
Guess what happens next?
They come back to you
I have always wondered what I would do if I saw you again
But damn who knew?

Some time has passed and I haven't seen you in a while
As you can see, I'm all grown up now
So many pleasant memories came to the surface
At first I was nervous, and then excitement crept in
There was something special about seeing you
I spent all night wondering what is it
That makes me feel the bond we had deserves a revisit
I must say the good outweighs the bad
Looking back, I miss all that we had
I'm glad our paths have crossed at this point in my life
I've spent the last few years preparing to be a good man's wife
Are you that somebody?

We've had time to mature and gain stability
After all the time that's past, are you still feeling me?
Sometimes it takes all the things we go through
To find out your true love was right in front of you
Now we just know how to appreciate it
And I'm glad we've made it
So if love is blind, I don't ever want to see
As long as you are loving me for eternity

MEMORIES OF THAT NIGHT

I can't even begin to express how I feel
Memories of that night are so surreal
Long awaited, highly anticipated
And after one night, I'm left feeling more than elated
We played a game of touch and tease
You touch me here, I tease you there
Although we weren't alone, we did not seem to care
When I kissed your neck, you let out a soft moan
Your sensual caresses had me in a love zone
A true intimate moment, without it being too sexual
The way you held me close to you, let me know
You were thinking the same thing too
You would occasionally get that look in your eyes
That suggested we should take it to the next level
Curiosity maybe
I also sensed a hesitation that asked the question
Should we?
That night we laughed and danced
Blushed and held hands
Talked about whatever came to our minds
Never being too concerned with time
Although it was of the essence
My soul needed your presence
Now I'm reminiscing and wishing it can happen again
Then I'm reminded of the possibility that it may never be
Sadness creeps in
I cry, but in time I will be alright
As I forever have memories of that night

◯NCE UPON A STORM

Normally when he stops by, he and I stand outside and talk for a few. We both knew what will happen if we are alone for too long. This particular night, it was raining so hard. It was as if all of the angels in heaven were crying at the same time. When he called, I thought for sure he was going to say he wasn't coming. To my utmost surprise, I was amiss. He was calling to let me know he was pulling up outside so I could open the door. I rushed down the stairs like a kid on Christmas morning anticipating my kiss. I was more than excited. By the time he approached the door, he was soaking wet and so was I, although I hadn't even been outside.

When he got inside my house, his clothes were so wet, I offered to put them in the dryer. He declined. The more I insisted, the more he resisted. Then I suppose he realized he couldn't sit down on my sofa with those wet clothes; he finally agreed. I thought to myself, *yes indeed*! Reluctantly he pulled his shirt over his head revealing arms that must lift weights often. It had never taken me this long to get a man out of his clothes before. But somehow this was exciting. As he undressed, I would take a quick glance; patient yet anxious to get him out of his pants. I wonder, *What is his hesitation?* As the sound of thunder echoed, I jumped. He grabbed me in his arms as if to automatically protect me from any potential harm. Skin to skin, how do we fight the urge to give in and make love?

As my womanhood pulsates with anticipation, I let out a deep sigh. He stroked the back of my neck and look into my eyes. I bite my lip and shake my head no because it's too soon. He picks me up and carries me to my room, as if we are on our honeymoon. He lays me down on the bed and undresses me as lightning flickers creating a seductive ambiance. I'm not speaking but my body is begging for attention. Did I mention the assiduous man that he is? He gives me more than I can handle in one night; I'm too weak to put up a fight.

The passion was intense as his deep strokes left me feeling intoxicated; woozy. I remember thinking, *this feeling cannot end*. Something was definitely different with him. Am I in love? During this stormy night, his rhythm seemed to be in sync with the tune the raindrops played on my window. My body responded with a familiar melody causing our love making to be a beautiful symphony; once upon a storm.

BONUS POEMS

BLACK HISTORY IS AMERICAN HISTORY

The time has come to embrace reality
This country was built by individuals like you and me
A multicultural nation, so full of diversity
Black History is American History

Are you making a contribution? Are you leaving your mark?
In order to encourage someone else, you have to start
From within, to become a better person
In my opinion, there is nothing worse than
Self-hate, lack of passion, lack of self-esteem
Who said you couldn't fulfill your dream
Not Martin Luther King

I wish he was here to see how far we have come
But by no means are we done
We need to uplift our youth, give them the truth
Explain the significance of our history by showing living proof
That YES, your dreams too are within reach
Believing in yourself is what we need to teach
Making choices that will lead them to victory
Impacting, not just Black History, but American History

It's no mystery that success begins with the courage
To make a difference
For instance, my father once told me,
If at first you don't succeed, you best keep trying
What if Harriet Tubman gave up?
She went back nineteen times

As a small child, I was faced with tragedy
When I was ten years old, my mother was taken away from me
And although she died, I continued to be strong
Every day I pray when things go wrong, because they will
But still, I never lose hope
Even when I think I am at the end of my rope,
I get myself a new rope
This ain't a joke; we need to continue to strive
For excellence in order to better our lives

Everyday we need to reflect on the contributions of
African-Americans
Who had a dream, a thought, an epiphany
They took advantage of life's opportunities
So never mind the naysayers, dream that dream
My faith taught me:
"No eye has seen, no ear has heard, and no mind has imagined
What God's prepared for those who love Him."

Talent comes in so many forms
Never be afraid to deviate from the norm
Thinking outside the box and doing more than just existing
Stay true to who you are no matter the opposition
As far as competition, never down play your accomplishments
To protect the ego of another, my sisters and brothers
We have come a long way, but it's not over yet
A dream deferred can lead to a serious regret
Discover your purpose and guide your dreams into reality
Become not only a part of Black History but American
History!

$\mathcal{C}$ONVERSATION WITH GOD

Lord, I was watching the news today
And another one didn't make it
An innocent victim of gun violence, so I sit in silence
I don't understand

Lord, I got word that there was another innocent victim
She made it through but only fifteen years old
And now she's paralyzed, from the waist down
I don't understand

Lord, I don't understand because I don't know
How we are chosen?
How do you decide who stays and who goes?
I ask these questions because I want to make sense
Of my continued existence

As a survivor of gun violence
I want to know why you kept me here
It doesn't seem fair

Because, Lord, that little girl that was watching TV,
And playing with her doll didn't make it
That grandmother who was hanging curtains
In her own living room, didn't make it
And that little boy playing outside, didn't pull through
Although I prayed for his recovery

However, I made it and I feel guilty
Not only did I make it, I'm still standing
I have so many questions because I'm not understanding

My child:
Being God, I have to make some tough decisions
As to whom I call home and those I leave behind
For you, I have a purpose that you will understand in time
However, it's not about you, but what I will do through you

Very soon, the message I'm sending you will be clear
Trust in me, there is a reason why I kept you here
I have to keep this brief because I have others to tend to,
Those with far greater problems than you

Really, my Lord, like who?

Like those Hurricane Katrina victims, who are still displaced
How they were treated is a total disgrace
Even if it takes everything in Me
I will deliver them from that adversity
As for you, continue to be thankful for all that you have
Lean not on your own understanding and
Know that I am directing your path

Lord, I thank you and I no longer feel torn
I have finally accepted that on
That unforgettable day
I died and was immediately reborn
August 8, 2004

$\mathcal{A}$FTERWORD

I hope you have enjoyed *Moments in Love: Reflections through Poetic Expressions*. Self-disclosure is never easy. You have read some of my very personal and intimate thoughts but I hope you were inspired by at least one of my poems.

If you have purchased this poetry collection, thank you for your support. If you have borrowed this book to read for your personal enjoyment, thank you for your interest. Either way, please tell a friend!

Sincerely,

K. Lowery Moore,
Poet & Author

Share your thoughts with me by sending an email to
KLoweryMoore@aol.com

To schedule K. Lowery Moore for signings, book
events, book club discussion, poetry reading or
speaking engagements, please contact:

Lisa Smith, Author Relations
So Sophisticated Publications
LisaSmithPR@aol.com
(202) 903-5678

Don't forget the look for the novel, *When I'm Loving
You*, in bookstores everywhere. Visit the website:
www.authorsden.com/klowerymoore